My life as a goldfish

and other poems

Poems by
RACHEL ROONEY

Drawings by
ELLIE JENKINS

F
FRANCES LINCOLN
CHILDREN'S BOOKS

Contents

Wide Open

My magic eye sees the sticky beak of a baby chick
before the eggshell has broken.

It can catch the sun as it squints
and the stars as they wink at me.

My magic eye has discovered an unnamed planet
spinning at the edge of the galaxy.

It watches a woolly mammoth give her last sigh,
then sink gently beneath the ice.

My magic eye stares hard at the soft hairs
vibrating on an ant's belly.

If you have scribbled your secrets in a diary,
my magic eye will have read them.

Yesterday it spied on your nightmares
and tomorrow it will spy on your dreams.

My magic eye is wide, wide open.

Wolf Girl

Up from the woods a wolf-girl crept.
Silent, barefoot, lean and low.
Captured in midnight's frosted glow.

Found on a farmyard, hurried inside.
Scrubbed down by a fire, dried and clothed.
Fed hot pea soup lapped from a bowl.

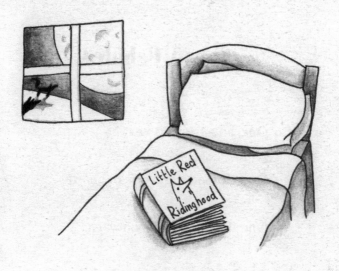

Taken upstairs to tell her the tale
of a wolf and a girl they'd once known.
Bolted the windows. Left her alone.

Safe in a room with a lamp and a bed,
wolf-girl curled in the lair of her robes,
howls for her brothers prowling the woods below.

Seven Pebbles

One, an egg – but heavier.

One crossed with veins of quartz.

One that might walk on water.

One to dip and raise to the light.

One that is heart-shaped.

One, with another one lodged inside.

Perfect pocket weights.

Raga Man

He's the ink's skin.
A rife fire.
A thin hint.
The lair liar.

He's the fort's frost.
He is part trap.
A lost slot.
The asp sap.

He's a loot tool.
The meat's steam.
The flue fuel.
An armed dream.

He's a plum's slump.
A saint stain.
He's got smug gums
and a bairn's brains.

Nobody Knows

Nobody knows what Jonjo knows. Nobody knows but he.
So Jonjo took me for a walk and showed his world to me.

I met him by the garden gate when the sun broke fresh and new.
Jonjo knows that fairies sleep on cobwebs laced with dew.

We strolled along the river's edge. It glistened in the light.
Sailing on a leafy boat, we saw a water sprite.

I followed him to forests and sank down to my knees.
Jonjo knows that wood elves meet in the hollow of old trees.

We climbed an icy mountain. Clouds drifted past our eyes.
There we spotted unicorns play chase across the skies.

I joined him at the ocean, where the mist rolled slowly in.
Jonjo knows a silver splash is the glimpse of a mermaid's fin.

He brought me to a stone cave as the sun began to fall,
to watch a dragon's shadow dance across the entrance wall.

We wandered in the starshine. An orange moon glowed bright.
Jonjo knows the man up there will keep us in his sight.

I got back home at midnight. He walked me to my door.
But as I turned to say goodbye, my Jonjo was no more.

Nobody knows what Jonjo knows. Nobody knows it's true.
So let me take you for a walk and I'll show his world to you.

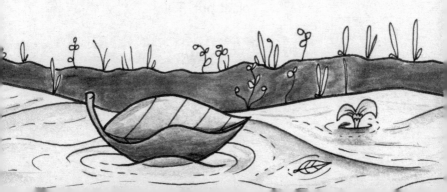

My Life as a Goldfish

T V	plant pot	books
T V	plant pot	books
T V	plant pot	books
TV	plant pot	books
plant pot	TV	books
plant pot	TV	books
plant pot	TV	books
plant pot	TV	books

CAT!

plant pot books

plant pot T V

plant pot books

plant pot T V

plant pot books

plant pot T V

CLAW!

Creature Speak

The Worm's Turn

I once lived with my owner
then he chose to set me free.
He fell down in that hole he dug
and now he lives with me.

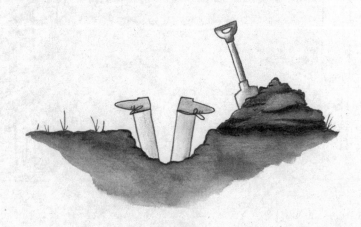

Lice are Nice

Head lice are not loners.
We're quite a friendly bunch.
That's why we swap our owners
when they sit down for their lunch.

Quiet Observation

If humans shed their skin, like us,
imagine how they'd moan and fuss.
And think of what a meal they'd make
when eating dinner like a snake.

Parrot's Complaint

Some people think
People think.

We're silly birds
Silly birds.

And so they teach us
So they teach us.

Silly words
Silly words.

Monkey See, Monkey Do

Monkey swing, monkey jump.
Monkey howl and monkey thump.
Monkey eat, monkey scratch.
Monkey throw and monkey catch.
Monkey see, monkey do.
Monkey me and monkey you.

Farewell Note

You called me a Slow Worm.
Well, I beg your pardon!
This quick moving lizard
has left for the garden.

Poems for Coldean School

Violet

Violet is a petal's face
that smiles from a porcelain vase.
It's the crinkling of paper foil
unwrapped from chocolate bars.

Violet is a lavender sniff
that tingles inside your nose.
It's the swish of silk from a royal cloak
touching the top of your toes.

Violet is the fizz of a sweet
dissolving on your tongue.
And it's the words I wrote for Violet class
whose poems have just begun.

Indigo

Indigo is the curve of a bridge
that holds the rainbow's light.
It's the padding paws of a feral cat
as she tiptoes through the night.

Indigo is the petrol haze
on a busy city street.
It's the brush of a velvet pillowcase
against a sleeping cheek.

Indigo is a Ribena slurp
sucked from a straw in a glass.
And Indigo is the ink that wrote
the poem for Indigo class.

Flame

Fire under footfall.
Fire over skies.

Fire on a matchstick.
Fire in my eyes.

Fire holding hunger.
Fire seeking wood.

Fire hiding danger.
Fire feeling good.

Fire as the enemy.
Fire acting friend.

Fire I must stamp on.
Fire I must tend.

Fire in the embers.
Fire at the heart.

Fires to remember.
Fires yet to start.

The Whisper

Don't be dim! teased the lamp.
I can keep the dark away.
My 60 watt bulb's not afraid.
You'll see – I'll make your day.

Psst, quick! hissed the microwave.
Grab a meal, in a tick.
Feast or snack, take your pick.
It's only a click and a ping away.

Over here! the radiators piped.
We'll heat you right. No fuss
when we're around. Trust us,
you'll be safe and sound tonight.

But the half-hot girl
chewing half-burnt toast
gazing into the ghostly flames,
heard a whisper, *Stay close, stay close.*

And she did.

Six Facts About Light

At dawn, she climbs over the horizon
to slink between the curtains
and rest her head on your pillow.

You might meet her in a forest gap
growing foxgloves,
or waiting at the exit of a long, concrete tunnel.

Her gaze could scorch your drawings,
set light to the hay,
blind inquisitive eyes.

Sometimes, in summer,
she'll reveal the lucky stripes
in the lining of her raincoat.

She can bounce off a full moon
and land softly at your feet
before you have counted to two.

On foggy nights, when the bare bulb
blows in an empty room, she is still there.
Blinking in the darkness, like an idea.

Birthday

Wind was angry,
slammed the door.
Smash went the glass
on the kitchen floor.

Out in the garden
Wind shook trees.
Kicked up a fuss
and a pile of leaves.

Wind was howling,
started to shout.
*Who blew the candles
on my birthday cake out?*

Liar

I told a whopper, a fib, a lie.
Slipped out of my mouth. It was slimy, sly.

Save me, it hissed. *A secret must hide.*
So I opened my bag and it slithered inside.

It fed in the dark, grew fat on my shame
as I carried it with me. It whispered my name.

My friend, it kept saying, *there's no need to frown.*
But that load on my shoulder was dragging me down.

It wouldn't stay still and it started to smell.
I stumbled and tripped on my words. I fell.

In horror, I watched as my lie tumbled out.
Down by my feet it lay, wriggling about.

A crowd gathered round. They let out a cry
It's a lie. It's a lie. It's a lie. It's a lie.

It is. I admit it, I quietly replied.
And the lie took a last gasp, shrivelled and died.

Making Friends

A new boy joined our class today.
His eyes are red, his skin is grey.
He will not come outside to play.
I think he needs a friend.

We set the goalposts on the grass.
We pick our teams, we strike, we pass.
He's watching from behind the glass.
I'm sure he wants a friend.

A tackle causes injury,
some blood is trickling from my knee.
I limp to class and there I see
the boy who has no friend.

He greets me with a sharp-toothed grin.
He licks his lips and helps me in.
Did I just hear him whispering?
Now you shall be my friend.

What am I?

Line
Dot

Cold
Warmer
Hot!

Misunderstandings

SHAKE BEFORE OPENING
read the bottle of juice.
So gave it a go
but my head came loose.

Adults like to spoil our fun.
I find it quite dismaying.
They even write it in the streets
SLOW DOWN CHILDREN PLAYING.

NO BALL GAMES ALLOWED

the notice said.
So I bounced it quietly
on my head.

Cheer Up

Give me a smile
with lips stretched wide as a rubber band
and in between a set of straight white teeth
dazzling like a mirror ball.

I promise not to lose that smile.
I'll hold it tight and deep
down a handy pocket
in a wipeable moon-shaped case.

My smile will be looked after well.
I'll scrub and floss it, preventing rot
and rub its skin with cocoa butter
to stop the cracks.

I'll save my smile for special occasions:
school photographs, when everyone laughs
at jokes that I don't get. Or just to prove
I didn't cry when my team lost.

I'll grab that smile and stick it on
so quick they won't discover
the other one I'm trying to hide.
The smile that's hanging upside down.

Monday Morning

Hot head. Mum tuts.
Into bed. No buts.
Fresh sheets. Warm drink.
Want a treat. Mum winks.
Fake sleep. Mum goes.
Sneaky peep. Tiptoes.
Channel flick. Key turns.
Up quick. Mum returns.
Knocks twice. Here we go.
Choc-ice. Beano.
Head felt. Asked how
temperature normal now.
Later on, practise cough.
(Radiator turned off.)

We Wish You a Hairy Kiss, Miss

(To the tune – *We Wish You a Merry Christmas*)

We wish you a hairy kiss, Miss.
We wish you a hairy kiss, Miss.
We wish you a hairy kiss, Miss.
And a bottle of beer.

Good tie strings we bring
to you and your bin.
We wish you a hairy kiss, Miss.
And a bottle of beer.

A Song to Annoy Adults when Visiting a Museum

(To the tune – *Oh I Do Like To Be Beside the Seaside*)

Oh I do want to be inside the gift shop.
Oh I do want to be inside the shop.
Oh I do want to wander down the aisles, aisles, aisles
where the toys mount up in colourful piles, piles, piles.
I'll behave when I get inside the gift shop.
When I'm inside, this stupid song will stop.
If you let me join the queue
for a souvenir or two
inside the gift shop, inside the shop.

Mrs Von Pugh

Let me tell you the story of Mrs Von Pugh,
a teacher so fierce she could scare off the flu.
Her hair's like a jungle. I'm sure that a crow
could nest there all summer and no one would know.

Her eyes are quite beady, like little squashed flies,
but they work even better than highly trained spies.
Even when she is standing, her back to the class,
she sees all the scribbly notes that we pass.

Her ears are like radar, they hear every sound
from whispers and giggles to worms in the ground.
Her nose knows exactly which smell comes from who.
She can sniff out a sweet from ten metres – it's true.

The work that she gives us would baffle Einstein
like the square root of sixteen, divided by nine
times three, add on twenty. And that's just the start.
We then have to learn all the school rules by heart.

And if we dare break one, we pay for our crime
by spending a week doing Maths at playtime.
You may think I'm lying, just messing about.
I don't need to prove it, I'll let you find out.

Our teacher is leaving – yes, Mrs Von Pugh
has a job at your school, in your classroom. With you.

The Answer

What words are teasing,
annoying, displeasing?
What's sure to put you in a stew?
What makes you cross
when your brain's at a loss
for the answer?

(I'm not telling you.)

The Problem with Spelling

It really doesn't help at all
to break up every silly ball.
Because, you see, the problem is
that syllable is spelt like this.

Ears cannot hear the ear in heard
so sounding out each word's absurd.
I write, I rub, I write and then
I cross it out and start again.

Just look it up! the teachers roar.
That's what the dictionary's for.
But I just end up in a mess
'cos psychic doesn't start with S.

So now I use the class computer,
more useful than a private tutor.
It checks out every word I spell
and nose eye can right sum things well.

Home Time

It's five past three.
Sixty-four eyes look at me.
No. Sixty-two.
Not Matthew.
He hasn't learnt to read my face.
He's got digital. A disgrace!
I reach to ten.
The school bell sounds and then – relief.
No more glueing, sticking.
Just me and the teacher
ticking
ticking
ticking.

The 20a Bus

(Written aged 10½)

In the line you hear a chatter.
Up and down a clatter, clatter.
Noisy schoolgirls scream and shout,
pushing in and pushing out.

Down the street the red bus trundles.
Girls surge forward all in bundles.
On at last, but what a rush,
banged my elbows in the crush.

I don't know what it's coming to!
said the lady with big buttons, who
had a habit to pursue
the trivial things young children do.

And when the bus stops in the street
I kick her underneath the seat.
And when the lady stops her chat
I pull the cherries from her hat.

The Inspection

The day the inspectors turned up here,
we knew it was going to be tough.
The problem was that our behaviour
was simply not dreadful enough.

The headless headmaster took action.
He hatched out a plan for the school,
and passed it around in a leaflet
entitled **GUIDELINES FOR THE GHOUL**.

Your wailing is weak and infrequent.
Your walking through walls could improve.
I'd like to hear more creaking handles,
I'd like to see more objects move.

You must make more effort to vanish.
At least, slowly fade out from sight.
I don't want to see you in lessons
unless your appearance is right.

The way that you play in the playground
is really not shocking me much.
Try harder to creep up on classmates
and grab with a cold, clammy touch.

In PE you must wear the full kit
so here's a reminder once more:
just slip on a white sheet with eye holes
and chains that reach down to the floor.

We followed these guidelines with gusto
each time the inspectors were there.
The head (and his body) was dead pleased,
he literally floated on air.

We thought they'd be here until Friday,
but on Monday at quarter to two
they ran out the school gates in terror.
I think we impressed them. Don't you?

Tea

A hungry boy from 10 AC
8 some letters and numbers for T
When asked simply Why?
they heard him reply
G U812 – just like me!

Monster's Lunch

Give me
french flies
grated bees
scabetti hoops in sores
lice-cream
with fresh newt salad for my pudding.
Or
scrambled legs
beans on toes
flesh finger
served with lips.
And after that
a bowl of bog-dirt.

Anything but chips.

Superstitious Sayings

Step on a crack,
Break your mother's back.
(Trip on a stone.
Break your own.)

See a penny, pick it up.
All the day you'll have good luck.
(Keep on looking, lucky kid.
Hopefully you'll find a quid.)

An apple a day
Keeps the doctor away.
(Unless you're a pet.
Then it's the vet.)

Never Never Never

Wear wellies when you're swimming
or put jelly in your hair,
brush your teeth with chilli pepper
or tease a grizzly bear.

Don't ever think of sitting
on a mountain of red ants.
Unless of course you want to learn
the itchy-scratchy dance.

Don't put stickers on your knickers,
they'll come off in the wash.
And never ask a hippo
for a friendly game of squash.

Playing catch with your dad's cactus
is really not that clever.
Oh, and sniffing his old trainers
is another triple never.

You can ignore these warnings
but there's one thing you should know.
There's nothing more annoying
than the words *I told you so!*

Nursery Rhyme Adverts

Property for Sale

Two houses up for sale.
One stick, one straw.
Both self-assembly.
See pig next door.

Lonely Heart

Handsome, lean wolf,
likes acting and cooking.
Tired of old grannies,
is currently looking
for lady in red
with plump and soft skin
to share walks in the forest
and cosy nights in.

Epitaph for Humpty Dumpty

Beneath this stone there lies a shell
of someone who had talents.
But (as you can probably tell)
one of them wasn't balance.

Touching Wood

Plastic's fantastic
and glass is first class.
Fabric, metal and stone are appealing.
But when saying *Touch Wood*
for good luck, then you should
make sure wood is the thing you are feeling.

Don't Move the Goalposts

Don't move the goalposts.
Leave them as they are.

Well, maybe this much wider.
Now you've gone too far.

In a bit more. Stop.
OK, that'll do.

No! You can't wear your jumper
unless you swap it for a shoe.

What d'you mean you're cold now?
You always have to moan.

Don't go. I didn't mean it.
I can't play on my own.

Trees will be Trees

A tree swung on a little boy,
as trees are prone to do.
They don't mean to be rough
but boys aren't that tough,
and it snapped his arm in two.

Dead Sea

You won't find fishes in the Dead Sea.
It really is dead boring.
There's just water, plenty of salt
and the occasional tourist, snoring.

A Sad Ending

A cynical man from Mauritius
thought it foolish to be superstitious.
When a black cat passed near
he stood firm, without fear.
(What a shame that the panther was vicious.)

Prayer

I lit a candle
and said a prayer
for everyone,
everything,
everywhere.

Then after that
I lit another.
And prayed for a rat
or a baby brother.

My Love is Like Chad Muska

I really cannot stand this stuff,
this mushy hearts and flowers guff.
My love is like a red, red rose...
Pur-lease.

Now, I'm not averse to verse,
don't get me wrong, there's worse.
But this gets up my nose.
It makes me sneeze.

So if you need to liken me
to something, via poetry,
remember this – I'm not some Romeo.
Give me talk of Tony Hawk or
say I'm like that skateboard pro, Chad Muska,
when you see me take a cool 5-0.

Try, *Your Tail Grab really grabs me*
Your Three Sixty Flip just grips me.
When I watch you on the half pipe,
it's a laugh. Yeah, you're just my type.

Something like that would be all right,
I suppose.
You might even get a name check.
Get a chance to flex on my deck.
And then later on...
Well, later on...who knows?

The Bench

I carved the letters deep, with pride.
I scarred the polished pine.
And now we lie here side by side,
your first name touching mine.

The rain may fade my traces
and the frost may blur your form.
But couples in embraces
will keep our winters warm.

Stone

(For Gerard Benson)

Stone remembers sea: its salty lap.
Sea remembers river's winding map.

River remembers leaf: a thickening.
Leaf remembers sun's awakening.

Sun remembers moon: its darker side.
Moon remembers stone, and brings the tide.

Wall

He sits in the damp shade
with his thoughts, his back to the wall.
And that football's heavy thud
against brick – and their laughter.

He makes lists of the creatures
that hide behind climbers, in crevices:
woodlice, spiders, aphids and snails.
Calculates their number in hundreds.

He sits with his back to the wall,
imagines himself painting it.
Names in his head the colours he'd mix:
moss green, burnt sienna, ochre.

Chick

She was born on the first day of spring
in a nest lined with words.
Met by the squabble of sisters,
long sermons at church.

Laid in a cradle of paper,
she rocked with its beat.
Awoke to a chorus of voices,
the pattering of feet.

Spoon fed with proverbs, mottos,
she swallowed them all.
Followed by ink from a bottle,
sucked up through a straw.

Sent to a school that taught daydreams,
wishing, white lies.
Grew wings. Taught herself how to sing.
Disappeared in the sky.

X

At the heart of the forest is a buried chest,
full to the brim with finished things:

all those fingers crossed, a first-aid box,
wrong answers marked, my faded flag,

the trail of planes on an August day,
that cartwheel trick and a single kiss.

I've got a map. I know exactly
where X is – and what. It marks the spot.

Magic

Magic   slips
between   the
cracks   in
real   life.
One   day
you   will
step   on
    it.

RACHEL ROONEY trained as a special needs teacher and currently works with children with Autistic Spectrum Condition. She also leads workshops in schools as a visiting poet. She has been shortlisted for the Belmont Poetry Prize, commended in the 2010 Escalator poetry competition, and 60 of her poems have been published in children's poetry anthologies. She won the 2012 CLPE Poetry Prize for her first solo children's collection, *The Language of Cat*. She lives in Brighton.

WINNER OF THE CLPE POETRY PRIZE 2012

978-1-84780-167-8

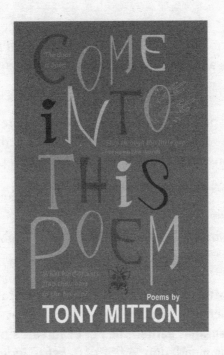

Poems by
TONY MITTON

978-1-84780-169-2

'Revel in the powerful and evocative language of this
collection. Wonderful for extending the imagination
and inspiring children to 'think outside the box'.'
– *Parents in Touch*

978-1-84780-452-5

Find out the mysterious rules of Werewolf Club, how to look like a rainbow, what happens when puppies fall in love – and how to fold up your gran! This is an exciting debut poetry collection from a young poet who is already performing his work successfully at venues across the UK.

978-1-84780-365-8
Shortlisted for the CLPE Poetry Prize 2014

'Lovely to read aloud with catchy rhymes and topics
guaranteed to appeal to children. The language is
vivid and some of the poems end in an unexpected
way that will make children giggle.'
– *Parents in Touch*

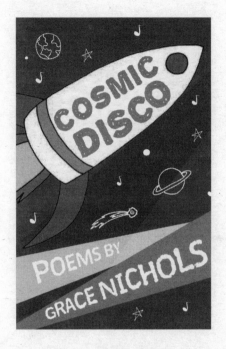

978-1-84780-398-6
Shortlisted for the CLPE Poetry Prize 2014

'Award-winning Grace Nichols creates all the moods
evoked by the title in this beautiful anthology which
lightly captures the wonder of the world … Every poem
is a delight in itself while together they give readers
a newly painted world.' – *Love Reading*